DEAL
IN OLD PHOTOGRAPHS

COLLECTED BY
JUNE BROADY

ALAN SUTTON
1989

Alan Sutton Publishing
Gloucester

First published 1989

British Library Cataloguing in Publication Data

Deal in old photographs.
1. Kent, history
I. Broady, J.
942.2'3

ISBN 0-86299-675-9

DEDICATION

To my daughter Dianne who lives so far away in Canada but still regards Deal as home.

Typesetting and origination by
Alan Sutton Publishing
Printed in Great Britain by
Dotesios Printers Limited

DEAL
IN OLD PHOTOGRAPHS

INTRODUCTION

The name 'Deal' is said to come from the Saxon 'Dylk' meaning a low lying or marshy place. Deal is a friendly town, a small town and an ancient town. Indeed, its history dates back some 4,000 years. The high ground to the south west of Deal was first settled by neolithic man and in recent years many tools, weapons and pottery have been excavated. This area was also chosen for settlement by men of the Bronze Age, and in the countryside around Deal typical round burial barrows of that period can be seen. Later, in 55 BC, Julius Ceasar made his first attempt to colonise England when he landed somewhere between Walmer and Deal. There is also reference to Deal in the Domesday Book, as Addelam in the Hundreds of Beusburg and Cornelei, although very little now remains of Norman Deal. The importance of Deal grew and in 1229 it became incorporated as a member of the Cinque Port of Sandwich, whereby it was responsible for providing men and materials, and ships, as a bulwark against invasion.

Deal has three castles within its boundaries, built in the shape of a Tudor Rose by Henry VIII in 1530 and each a mile apart, at Sandown, Deal and Walmer. They were built as a line of defence against invasion by the French and Spanish, for Henry, having angered the Pope through his insistence upon a divorce from Catherine, was fearful of attack. However, the occasion never arose and the only time they can be said to have been used in anger was against Cromwell's Army in 1648. Sandown later served as a prison for Colonel John Hutchinson who had signed the death warrant of Charles I. Sadly, only a few ruins remain of this castle. Early in the eighteenth century Walmer Castle became the official residence of the Lord Warden of the Cinque Ports. Many illustrious people have served in this capacity, the most notable among them have been William Pitt, the Duke of Wellington, who died there in 1852 and more recently Sir Winston Churchill and Sir Robert Menzies. The present holder of the office is Queen Elizabeth the Queen Mother. Deal Castle is the largest of the three, with walls 20 feet thick at the base, and it may be regarded as the finest surviving of those castles built by Henry. Major General Iain Harrison RM is the present Captain of the Castle, a sinecure conferred upon him by the Queen.

The Duke of Albany's Maritime Regiment of Foot (the Admiral's Regiment) was established in Deal in 1665. The title Royal Marines was conferred on them by

George III. It was here that they trained to storm the Mole at Zeebrugge – an epic battle in which they showed great courage. Perhaps they should be regarded as the forerunners of the Commandos, for it was here at Deal that the first Commando Unit was formed in 1943. Not surprisingly they were accorded the honour of Freemen of the Town. The Royal Marine Band and Orchestra are known throughout the world. They are trained in the RM School of Music housed in the old Naval Hospital building in Deal where many a 'jolly Jack' was brought ashore after a naval engagement. The operating theatre, a gruesome place, still remains.

Deal was once the main harbour town of south-east England, a centre of marine activity. There was a naval yard stretching over many acres between the Castle and the Timeball Tower. Indeed, it might well be said that Deal was shaped by the sea. Sometimes there could be a hundred or more ships lying in the Downs, the stretch of water between the shore and the Goodwin Sands, while waiting for a fair wind to carry them down the Channel. All needed to be provisioned with fresh meat, vegetables and flour and Deal boatmen were kept busy, plying their galley punts and luggers to and fro with these goods and with passengers. There was always a large number of seamen in the town while their ships were being serviced and every other building along Beach Street seems to have been an ale house or hostelry. Unfortunately this led to the town getting a bad reputation – Cobbett regarded it as 'a most villanous place, full of filthy looking people'. As might be supposed, a great deal of smuggling was carried on for, with its wide open beach, it was easy for small boats to come ashore laden with their contraband of brandy, silk or lace. Many of the old houses are said to have been hideouts for smuggled goods. Sadly, some were destroyed by enemy action during the war and, more recently, some have been demolished to make way for 'modern improvement'. But much still remains and hopefully, with conservation, will continue to do so.

The earliest recorded incident of smuggling was in 1617 when 'owlers' – midnight adventurers – were surprised by revenue men and their goods of raw wool, which they were trying to load into a Dutch vessel, were confiscated. However, during the eighteenth century Deal smugglers really came into their own. The Napoleonic wars caused high duties to be levied and this made imported smuggled goods much more profitable; considerable gain could also be had from gold smuggled into French ports and a blind eye was turned upon their activities in return for the information they could bring back from the Continent. The Deal boatmen's reputation as seamen was particularly high at that time but following the end of the Napoleonic war their usefulness as couriers was over. William Pitt, in order to conclude smuggling activities, ordered the firing of all local boats drawn up on the beach one January morning in 1784 – a mortal blow to boatmen as it was the destruction of their only means of livelihood.

The Timeball Tower, the first in a chain of semaphore stations by which messages could be relayed from Deal to London, was built towards the end of the eighteenth ✕ century. Following the invention of telephone and radio it fell into disrepair but in recent years it has been lovingly restored and is in full working order.

The notorious Goodwin Sands, lying about four miles offshore and stretching for about ten miles along the coast, are responsible for the loss of hundreds of ships and cargoes. Sometimes on a clear day their ghostly masts can be seen rising from the water. Many tales are told about phantom sightings and one such is that of the *Lady Luvibund*. In fair winds, on 13 February 1748 the *Lady Luvibund* steered a promising course down Channel for Oporto with her cargo and, more importantly, Captain Simon Read's new bride, Anetta, her mother and their wedding guests. However, the ship's Mate John Rivers was to have married Anetta and, vengeful for the loss of his intended, he brained the helmsman and ran the sailing ship onto the Goodwin Sands. The merry party in the cabin, deaf to imminent destruction, was finally aroused by sounds of pounding seas, snapping timbers and Rivers' idiot laughter as the *Lady Luvibund* was drawn down.

The *Lady Luvibund* did not rest. Forty years later on 13 February 1798 Captain James Westlake of the *Edenbridge*, warily passing the sands, was nearly run down by an unidentified sailing ship which, in proper spectral manner, sheered nimbly past to shouts of drunken laughter from below. Westlake found that local fishermen, sufficiently persuaded of her substance to search for survivors of the wreck, had found nothing. In 1848 the 'hovellers' of Deal (*inter alia* fishermen, smugglers and salvagers) again caught sight of the strange ship and put out to her aid. No trace was found. Again, without physical clue, she was seen on 13 February 1898. The superstitious waited for 1948 but, disappointingly, in that memorial year the *Lady Luvibund* remained invisible. Although, in a far-fetched attempt to match her with the supernatural at all costs, some discovered her hand in the wreck of the *Silvia Onorato* on the Goodwins, saying that instead of making a personal appearance she had claimed a sacrifice. (Taken from *Folklore of the Sea* by Margaret Baker.)

St Leonards Church, lying in Upper Deal a mile from the town, is the parish church of the town, part of it dating from the thirteenth century. A red brick tower topped by a white cupola was erected in 1684 and the north aisle was enlarged in 1819. It has galleries around three sides, the one at the west end being 'Built by Ye Pilots of Deal' so that they could come and go with the tide without disturbing the congregation.

In the town itself stands the fine red brick civic Church of St George the Martyr, built in 1716 as a chapel of ease. Captain Parker, Nelson's friend, died in Deal and was buried in the churchyard. Nelson attended the funeral and is said to have leant against a tree and wept, but no-one is sure which tree. During the shelling of Deal in the Second World War the east window above the altar was shattered, and only one piece remained in position bearing the word 'Hope'. That piece still remains, having been incorporated into the new window depicting the lifeboat on a mission of mercy.

As well as having three castles, Deal is unique in having had three lifeboat stations; North Deal, Kingsdown and Walmer. Only Walmer station remains in operation. Here the lifeboat sits on a cradle at the top of the beach. If the need arises it is launched in a few minutes down the beach over baulks of greased timber; a most impressive and exciting sight to witness. Walmer also has an inshore lifeboat which is kept in the eighteenth-century boathouse. Across the road, The Strand, stands the lifeboatmen's church of St Saviours. Walmer, originally a medieval village, has a twelfth-century church which was built as a chapel to Walmer Castle. The new church of St Mary's, built on high ground, now serves the people of Walmer.

In an attempt to encourage visitors and to combat the decline in the town's prosperity a regatta was staged in 1826. It was a great success, men and boats coming from far away to compete and the regatta ended with a firework display. The regatta is still an annual event, usually taking place during the third week of July.

When excavations for a Channel Tunnel were stopped in 1882 the workings at Shakespeare Cliff at Dover provided a base from which to bore for coal and by 1900 there were several pits in East Kent. Two of them, Tilmanstone and Betteshanger, particularly affected Deal. Miners with their families came from Wales, Durham and Scotland to work at the coal face. Hundreds of houses were built and communities formed. They are still as parochial today as they were all those years ago. Tilmanstone and Betteshanger have now closed.

The railway came to Deal on 15 June 1881 when the London, Chatham and Dover Company opened their extended line from Dover to Deal. The official opening was attended by 250 invited guests who had travelled from other parts of Kent to Dover where they boarded a special train. The Mayor and Corporation of Deal waited on the gaily decorated platform at Deal to welcome the Directors of the railway company. To cater for the number of holidaymakers who travelled to Deal by train the South Eastern Railway Company commissioned the designing and building of a luxury hotel in 1886 – The South Eastern Terminus Hotel and two years later it was opened to the public. Later it became known as 'The Queens'. Sadly it closed its doors in 1977 and in 1981 it was completely destroyed by fire.

It became expedient for the town to have a police force and by 1857 this consisted of a sergeant and three constables full time with two part-time constables who assisted on night duty. At that time the police station was located in the Town Hall. By 1865, following the recommendation of the Inspector of Constabulary, an additional sergeant and three constables were appointed headed by a superintendent. On 1 August 1889 the Deal Borough Police Force was merged with the Kent County Constabulary. It was here that the author's husband served six years as the Officer-in-Charge.

A new Coat of Arms was granted to the town in 1966, the shield still bearing the three demi lions passant and three hulls of the Cinque Ports, surmounted by a silver oar. Above the shield were added a castle and on either side supporters – a Roman centurion (dexter) and a Royal Marine (sinister). The Town's motto is *Adjuvate Advenas* (Befriend the Stranger) and visitors to Deal will, I am sure, always receive a warm welcome.

POINTS OF REFERENCE

Bulwark Shore by Caroline Hillier.
Folklore of the Sea by Margaret Baker.
King's England (Kent) by Arthur Mee.
Museum Archives.
Deal & Walmer History Society notes.

PHOTOGRAPHS

The Will Honey Collection (now housed in the Martime & Local History Museum). Mrs Joan Marriott, Miss Julie Dellar. I acknowledge the assistance given by Director of the Museum, Mr Colin Dalton, and the Chairman of the Trustees, Capt. J. Brown.

AN AERIAL VIEW of Deal castle.

DEAL CASTLE from the road.

THE GATEWAY to Deal castle.

THE OLD TOLLGATE, Upper Deal, early this century.

ST LEONARD'S – the Parish Church of Deal – bears signs of its Norman origin, although greatly altered in the seventeenth century. It has a painted western gallery dated 1705 and inscribed 'This gallery was built by ye Pilots of Deal'. The western tower of brick dates from 1684 and the chancel, with very fine sedilia, is of the thirteenth century.

ANOTHER VIEW of St Leonard's Church.

THE OLD MANOR HOUSE, a fine building in Upper Deal. Now demolished.

KEPPEL COTTAGE, Upper Deal. Admiral Keppel, First Lord of the Admiralty, gave his name to one of Deal's oldest hostelries.

THE LONDON ROAD AND MANOR ROAD JUNCTION, Upper Deal. Jenkins Well, a seventeenth-century house, is on the corner and the small white building is now a garage for the big house. The house next door has been demolished and two others built in its place.

UPPER DEAL HOUSE on the right. The house facing it is Jenkins Well.

THE OLD MILL HOUSE, at the top of Mill Hill, was the last of Deal's mills to be demolished in 1929. It had replaced an earlier post mill of the eighteenth century. Mill Hill came by its name because of the two mills which stood in the area; Wellington Mill at the foot and Upper Mill at the top.

THE TOWN GOLF MILL in 1897 – the miller was a Mr C.W. English.

SANDOWN CASTLE.

ANOTHER VIEW of Sandown Castle. The small notice warns people that they would be 'proceeded against as the law directs' if caught taking beach sands, flints or boulders.

SANDOWN CASTLE — note the shattered wall in the foreground.

WALMER CASTLE AND GARDENS which were designed by Lady Hester Stanhope, niece of William Pitt who was Lord Warden of the Cinque Ports and often stayed at the castle; his official residence.

TAKING PART IN A PAGEANT at Walmer Castle in 1949 are Barbara Godfrey (now Cox) and Margaret Cooper.

TWO VERY FAMOUS MEN had connections with Deal and Walmer. The Duke of Wellington was Lord Warden of the Cinque Ports and often stayed at Walmer Castle, his official residence, where he spent many hours looking over the battlements towards France. There is a small museum where one can see the original Wellington boots, his reading desk, camp bed and the armchair in which he died. Admiral Lord Nelson often came ashore when his ship was anchored in the Downs.

THE GREAT HOUSE at Walmer – Walmer Place.

RUINS of the old Norman Manor House, Walmer.

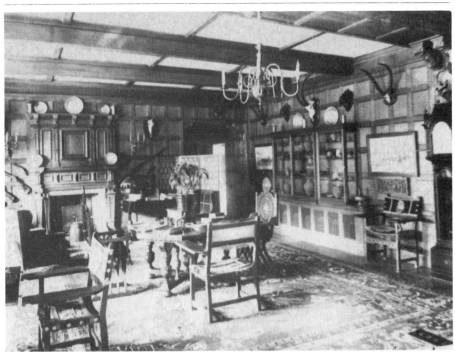

INSIDE THE HALL — Roman remains on show here were dug up in the grounds.

WALMER PLACE — the Flower Walk.

GOTHIC HOUSE, Walmer – home of Lady Woolaston.

ST MARY'S, the new parish church of Walmer, with a fine tower.

THE OLD WELL, Walmer.

OLD ST MARY'S CHURCH, Walmer. The church has a magnificent Norman chancel, a fourteenth-century picena and fifteenth-century panels in the reredos.

ST SAVIOUR'S CHURCH, The Strand, Walmer – the Lifeboatmen's Church. The lifeboat house (a listed building) with the weathervane stands across the road.

AN AERIAL VIEW of Walmer Lifeboat Station. The lifeboat sits in a cradle at the top of the beach. When needed, the head launcher knocks out the shackle pin and the boat speeds down the beach over baulks of timber to the water.

DEDICATION of Walmer lifeboat, *Charles Dibdin*, Civil Service No. 32 on 25 July 1959.

THE HAMPSHIRE ROSE on service.

SOS SIGNALS from the direction of *Gull* Lightship were heard at 3.50 a.m. on 17 March 1929. The crew of Deal motor boat *Lady Beatty* mustered – Harry Meakins, Charlie Pritchard, David Pritchard, Edward Griggs, Dick Brown and Tommy Baker – and the boat was launched at 4.10 a.m. They proceeded in dense fog in the direction of *Gull* lightship and found that the SOS was coming from the *City of York*, bound for London with a pilot aboard, that had run into the sunken lightship and was at anchor. The crew of the lightship had been taken aboard but the Master was missing. The motor boat *Terrier* and the Ramsgate lifeboat arrived and a search was instituted, but he was not found. *Lady Beatty* returned to Deal but was immediately sent back to stand by the sunken lightship until relieved by Trinity House tender *Satellite*, this time equipped with an old sailing ship's fog signal, extra flares and a large ship's bell. On locating the sunken lightship the daylight showed that the cage on top of the mast was above water. Dick Brown spent several hours in this cage from which he rang the bell whenever vessels were approaching; several vessels were saved from going ashore on the Goodwins due to the quiet bravery of these men. Relieved at four o'clock they arrived back at Deal at around six o'clock exhausted by their nerve-racking experience of 26 hours in an open boat in bad conditions. Twelve days later these same men were called upon to stand by the *S.Goodwin* lightship, which had been badly damaged, this time for 20 hours.

MR JAMES HALL OBE (affectionately known as 'Doc') with Coxswain, Freddy Upton. The OBE was awarded to Mr Hall in the King's Birthday Honours of 1946 in recognition of his self-sacrificing work throughout the war.

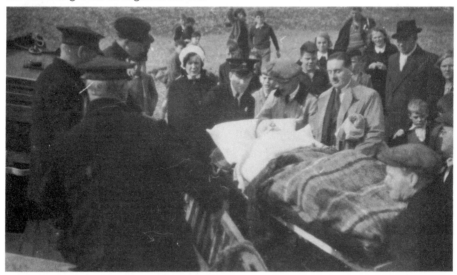

OCTOBER 1939. The doctor of the 10,000 ton Dutch liner *Nordam*, bound for New York, being returned to his ship by MV *Golden Spray* following an emergency operation performed by Mr Hall, the local surgeon and lifeboat doctor, who is here standing alongside his patient.

THE REVD THOMAS STANLEY TREUNOR, vicar of St George's Church for many years, chaplain to Missions for Seamen, the Downs, Honorary Secretary RNLI Walmer and author of *Heroes of the Goodwin Sands*.

RICHARD ROBERTS, Coxswain of the North Deal Lifeboat; one of the heroes the Revd Treunor wrote about.

THE CERTIFICATE OF SERVICE dated 13 June 1907, awarded to Richard Roberts for 22 years in the Lifeboat Service.

NORTH DEAL LIFEBOAT of which Richard Roberts was coxswain. Bonny Adams was coxswain during the First World War and the station closed when a motor lifeboat *Charles Dibdin* was placed at Walmer in July 1933.

PRESENTATION by US Naval Attaché, Capt. W.R. Sexton, on 3 July 1920, of medals for *Piave* rescue on 21 January 1919. Back row, left to right: William Wells, Frank Adams, Frank Budd, Sailor Jordan, Matt Hoile and Ernest May. Front row: Bonny Adams, Dido Redsull, Thomas Crillen, -?-, Benny May, tall civilian Mr Matthews of Thompsons Brewery, Sammy Trice, Richard Riley, Bob Holbourne and John Webb. In front is Lifeboat Secretary Prior and Capt. H.R. Sexton USN.

AN EARLY LIFEBOAT at Walmer.

CIVIL SERVICE No. 4 at Walmer.

FREDDY UPTON, George Dadd and 'Lardy' Dadd alongside the Walmer Lifeboat.

THE KINGSDOWN LIFEBOAT. This station also closed in July 1933 when the motor lifeboat *Charles Dibdin* was stationed at Walmer.

JARVIST ARNOLD, coxswain of Kingsdown Lifeboat and one of the *Heroes of the Goodwin Sands*.

THE PORTUGUESE SCHOONER *Flores* ashore at Walmer 12 January 1911. She was carrying a cargo of aniseed.

TOPSAIL SCHOONER *Robert Morris* of Caernarvon was driven ashore 31 December 1913 at Sandown Castle between 2 and 3 a.m. A northeasterly gale was blowing with squalls of hail and rain. She was towed off the same day, very leaky with loss of anchor and chain, and taken into Dover.

TWENTY VISITORS were trapped in St Margaret's Bay when, due to heavy snow, the village was cut off. They were brought back to Deal by the motor boat *Lady Hale* manned by Harry Meaking, Charlie and Dave Pritchard, Dick Brown and his son Jim.

BRITISH SHIP *Selscar* beached at Walmer 11 April 1949. Walmer Lifeboat *Charles Dibdin* attended for 61 hours. The vessel was badly holed when it collided with Swedish vessel *Nordic*. *Selscar* was later towed into Dover Harbour. Dick Brown of the lifeboat crew sustained badly damaged ribs while aboard *Selscar*.

SS *MAGNA* aground on the Goodwins.

SS *AGEN* aground on the sands on 13 January 1952. She was a French vessel of 4,186 tons with 35 crew and 2 passengers on passage from Hamburg to Dakar. Walmer lifeboat *Charles Dibdin* under the command of Coxswain Freddy Upton attended, rescuing all crew and passengers; a most arduous service lasting 11 hours. Freddy was awarded a bar to his silver medal and Percy Cavell, engineer, a bar to his bronze medal.

THREE PIERS are recorded as having been built at Deal. There is evidence that a pier or jetty was in existence from the end of the sixteenth century until the early nineteenth century. When schemes for the construction of a harbour at Deal came to nothing a company was formed in 1838 for the construction of a wooden pier. An Act of Parliament was obtained and Sir John Rennie designed a pier 445 ft long. Lack of funds probably accounted for the fact that only 230 ft were completed. This pier stood to the north of the Royal Hotel. It was blown down in a gale in 1857.

WITH THE MAYOR OF DEAL'S COMPLIMENTS.

7.S.Kennett
2 Wellfidt Road
Folkestone

An unique opportunity of seeing the BRITISH FLEET on a War Footing !

Visit of the Home Fleet
TO DEAL,

PRIOR TO NAVAL MANŒUVRES,

30th JUNE to 4th JULY, 1908.

On TUESDAY, 30th JUNE, 1908, the

Torpedo Flotilla of the Home Fleet,

Consisting of more than One Hundred Vessels,

Will arrive and anchor off Deal, and will leave again on Wednesday, 1st July.

On THURSDAY, 2nd JULY, 1908, the

Battle Ships and Cruisers of the Home Fleet,

THIRTY-EIGHT IN NUMBER,

Will arrive and remain at anchor in the Natural Harbour of the Downs off Deal and Walmer, until Saturday, 4th July, 1908.

Particulars showing Names, Descriptions, Horse-power of Engines, Number of Heavy Guns, and

PLAN OF STATIONS,

will be found overleaf.

T. F. PAIN & SONS, DEAL & SANDWICH.

ADVERTISING FOR A VISIT by the Home Fleet.

THE BATTLE FLEET assembled off Deal in 1910. The Downs, the stretch of water between the Goodwin Sands and the shore, provided safe anchorage.

THE SECOND PIER – built on the site of the present pier. The first column was put in place on 8 April 1863 and it was opened by the Mayor on 14 July 1864. This pier, built of iron, was 1,000 ft long. It was damaged on three occasions when ships were driven on to it. In January 1873 the barque *Merle* was driven through the supporting columns and another time the schooner *Alliance* collided with the pier occasioning some damage. Final damage was done on 29 January 1940 when the Dutch vessel *Nora* collided with the pier which collapsed under the impact. Prime Minister Winston Churchill visited Deal and ordered the demolition of the pier.

FISHING FROM THE PIER.

THE LADIES ANGLING CLUB gathered on the pier.

DEAL has always been a popular place for anglers. Here we see them taking part in an angling festival in 1930. Deal is probably the leading English centre, within easy reach of London, offering angling from beach, boat, pier and river.

GEORGE RIVERS, piermaster.

A NEW LIGHT FOR THE PIER. George Rivers, piermaster, at the top and 'Rumpty' Jarman at the bottom.

SS *NORA* colliding with the pier 29 January 1940.

WORK BEGAN on a new pier in 1954. Built of steel and encased in concrete it is 1,076 ft long.

DEAL PIER under construction.

PRINCE PHILLIP.

THE
CEREMONIAL
KEY

THE MAYOR, Councillor Sidney Stewart Dunn, presented His Highness with the ceremonial key to open the pier.

THE ROYAL MARINE BAND on parade in Queen Street on Tuesday 19 November 1957 for the opening of the new pier by HRH the Duke of Edinburgh. The Royal Marines were made Freemen of the Town on 4 February 1945, The Mayor (Ald. E.J. Dobson OBE) presenting a casket containing the certificate to General Hunton.

THIS 12 INCH CARTRIDGE CASE came from the Kaiser Wilhelm II Battery at Knocke, Belgium, which was in action on 23 April 1918. The beam from which it is suspended is part of the deck of HMS *Vindictive*. It was presented to the Royal Marines Depot at Deal, in memory of the gallant attack on Zeebrugge 22/23 April 1918, by Vice Admiral Sir Roger Keyes KCB KCVO CMG DSO. The man in khaki is Harry Stokes of Deal. Captain Bamford DSO RMA and Sgt. Finch RMA were awarded VCs after a ballot, but it was noted on records of all who took part that they had participated in a ballot for the VC.

THE ROYAL MARINES, headed by their band, returning from Church Parade through the Jubilee Gates.

THE PRINCE OF WALES, later Edward VIII, on a visit to the Royal Marine Barracks. The building behind the flagpole is the Officers' Mess. In the early evening of Tuesday 29 October 1940 enemy aircraft dropped bombs in front of the Mess, killing eight men.

THE ROYAL BUILDINGS and the Royal Marine School of Music (with clock tower), The Strand, Walmer.

THE ROYAL MARINES SCHOOL OF MUSIC – the rear (western) face – once East Barracks and the Naval Hospital.

ANOTHER VIEW of the western face – the operating theatre of the Royal Naval Hospital – now used as a store by the RM School of Music.

INSIDE THE OPERATING THEATRE showing the black marble operating table where many a sailor was brought following a battle.

SQUADRON 208 of the Royal Naval Air Service at Hawksdown, Walmer.

THE MEMORIAL at Hawksdown to the 15 pilots of No. 208 RNAS who lost their lives 1917/18 and who flew from this tiny airfield. The memorial was restored by 2235 Squadron ATC and rededicated on 26 April 1987.

TIMEBALL TOWER and gates to the Naval Yard which covered several acres between the castle and the Timeball Tower, and from the sea front some 100–150 yards back to Victoria Road.

ROBERT NEWBY, custodian of the Timeball Tower, 1870–74. He sailed in whaling ships in his younger days.

THE TIMEBALL TOWER showing its proximity to the house within the Naval Yard.

A CLOSER VIEW of the house where the Superintendant of the Yard lived with his family.

DEAL TOWN HALL, built on pillars like a market hall. The old gaol was at the back and the Council Chamber above. Quarter Sessions were held here until 1972. Deal was granted its Charter by William III on 13 October 1699.

ANOTHER VIEW OF THE TOWN HALL looking north along the High Street. Notice the water trough at the corner. The tree is in St George's churchyard.

FIRE ENGINES under the Town Hall, decorated for King George V's Silver Jubilee.

THE WALL of a much earlier Town Hall, behind Baldwin's Old Shop.

GUILDFORD HOUSE.

ADMIRALTY HOUSE, Queen Street, Deal, after its sale to the Odeon Cinema Co. showing the notice of sale.

HARTFIELD HOUSE, built in 1796, known as Percy T. Ransom's china shop.

QUEEN STREET before road widening.

GRIFFIN STREET. Notice the porthole squints at first floor and attic level.

TWO VIEWS OF PORTABELLA ALLEY taken from Middle Street on 29 October 1973.

THE MARINA CINEMA, Clarence Place. A row of new Georgian houses, at the College Road end of the High Street, now occupies the site.

THE INTERIOR of the Marina Cinema before 1911.

CUSTOM HOUSE LANE from Beach Street. The gate on the left is marked 59 Beach Street.

NAPIER TERRACE, Deal, in the 1880s.

THE JUNCTION OF WEST STREET and King Street, showing Royal House.

ROTHWELL HOUSE, opposite No. 1 Beach Street.

CROWN COURT looking east from the High Street.

THE OLD PLAYHOUSE in Middle Street.

DEAL HIGH STREET taken from Queen Street, facing north.

DEAL HIGH STREET from King Street to Queen Street, decorated for the Coronation of George V. White-Fullers outfitters are on the corner.

THE CHEQUERS INN – for years the only building on the ancient highway between Deal and Sandwich.

MR MARSH, Landlord of the Chequers public house.

A LATER VIEW of the Chequers — much work has been done on the building.

SEAGIRT HOUSE (now demolished) and the capstan to the north of the pier.

ROSWAY MANOR, Middle Deal Road.

CLANWILLIAM HOUSE, Walmer. The only house to remain on the beach at Walmer.

DEAL COLLEGE.

LLOYDS MEMORIAL CAXTON SEASIDE HOME opened 6 September 1911.

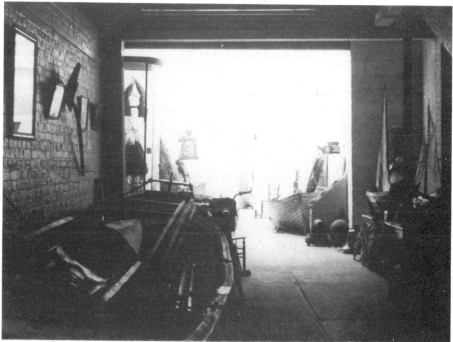

EARLY DAYS inside the Maritime and Local History Museum in St George's Road. There are a great many more exhibits on show now.

ROUND THE WORLD YACHTSMAN Sir Alec Rose and Lady Dorothy visiting the museum on 5 September 1975.

THE OFFICIAL OPENING of The Victoria Memorial Hospital 17 March 1924 by Prince Henry. Next to Prince Henry is Mr Redsull, former mayor and one time landlord of The Plough; the mayor was Mr Lambert of Lambert's Laundry and on the extreme right is Mr Solomon, also a former mayor.

THESE MODELS were found in an attic of a house in West Street, Deal, in 1957. They were restored for Deal Borough Council by Capt. Jim Brown (standing behind the models); also in the picture are Ald. Albert Cavell and a member of the Council staff. Both models are now safely housed in the Maritime and Local History Museum.

WINSTON CHURCHILL was installed as Lord Warden of the Cinque Ports on 14 August 1946 and became the thirteenth Freeman of the Borough of Deal on 15 August 1951; the ceremony was held before a gathering of nearly 1,000 people. The Certificate of Admission, in a silver casket, was presented by the mayor, Councillor F.F. Pottery, to Mr Churchill.

AN EARLY VISIT of Queen Elizabeth the Queen Mother to Deal. The Queen Mother is the present Lord Warden of the Cinque Ports with an official residence at Walmer Castle.

THE DUKE OF YORK, later King George VI, paying a visit to the Royal Marine Barracks at Walmer.

THE PROCLAMATION of King George V's accession in June 1910, outside St George's Church.

THE PROCLAMATION of Edward VIII's accession outside the Town Hall.

CORONATION FESTIVITIES in Gladstone Road, 1953.

THE CARNIVAL QUEEN'S CARRIAGE 31 August 1950. The carnival float was decorated entirely with flowers donated by Sholden Nurseries Ltd.

THE FIRST GPO PERSONALITY GIRL, 1960.

DEAL TELEPHONE EXCHANGE FLOAT at the 1959 carnival.

THE FIRST CARNIVAL FLOAT FROM DEAL TELEPHONE EXCHANGE, 1958

REGATTA AND CARNIVAL WEEK would not be complete without the fair held, in days gone by, along Deal sea front. The pier and Royal Hotel are visible in the background.

THE FAIR IS NOW HELD on Walmer Green.

THE START OF THE MARATHON, an annual event to Sandwich and back.

REGATTA WEEK — the Men's Flowerpot Race.

GALLEY PUNTS being launched from the beach. Galley punts vary in size between 21 and 30 ft in length and 7 ft beam. They carry one lug sail and a mast shipped well amidships.

THE RESCUE RACE – galley punts under sail.

MORRIS MEN performing a stick dance during Hop Hoodening – a custom to greet the harvest.

WALMER HOODEN HORSE.

North Deal.

ALONG NORTH DEAL SEA FRONT.

THE BEACH AND CENTRAL PARADE. Beach House (behind the shelter) is where it is said George II, having landed at Deal, rested on his return from Hanover in 1740 before journeying to London.

ANOTHER LOOK at the central parade and beach.

THE NORTH BEACH viewed from the pier. The Royal Hotel, now the only remaining one on the beach, was once called the Three Kings. It was where Lord Nelson stayed when the fleet was anchored in the Downs and where he could meet his beloved Emma. The rooms they occupied are still known as the Nelson and Hamilton rooms.

BOATS ON THE BEACH.

A CAT BOAT (a small lugger). *Early Morn* and her crew in 1876.

TAKING THE AIR and listening to the band.

VICTORIA PARADE — the tall building on the corner is the South Eastern, later the Queens Hotel.

LOW TIDE – playing bowls on the Goodwin Sands 13 July 1913. The remains of a wreck can be seen in the background.

PLAYING CRICKET on the sands. At low tide, when the sands are uncovered, they are, in parts, very firm but once covered with water they become quick sands and a man, or indeed a ship, can be sucked down very easily.

THIS BUILDING, constructed by the South Eastern Railway as a terminus hotel, later became the Queens Hotel. It has since been demolished following a fire. A block of luxury flats is now being built on the site.

THE OLD BREWERY occupied that corner of Stanhope Road and High Street from the post office to the Rose public house.

WALMER BREWERY and Yard (now demolished) 1915.

THE YARD OF T.T. DENNE WALMER, photographed for the *Deal and Walmer Illustrated*, 1897.

WILLIAM BONNY ADAMS, coxswain of North Deal Lifeboat during the First World War.

THE FUNERAL of Bonny Adams.

WILLIAM BONNY ADAMS' COFFIN followed by members of his crew.

THE NONCONFORMIST CHAPEL in Nelson Street. It later became an organ factory.

POLICEMAN No. 1 – James Shelvey Cox, the first 'Arm of the Law' in Deal.

PROCESSING PAST ST GEORGE'S CHURCH to the last Quarter Sessions to be held in Deal Town Hall in 1972. Leading the procession is Town Sergeant 'Jock' Cowie with the Town Mace, followed by the Recorder Sir James Percival KG QC, the Mayor Douglas Yates-Mercer, Clerk of the Peace Ronald Purnell (Town Clerk) followed by Chairman of the Magistrates Mr Charles Lock. Bringing up the rear is Chief Inspector Peter Broady who was the last Chief Inspector in charge of the Deal Sub-Division. It was later swallowed up in a much larger division.

THE FIRE BRIGADE outside the pastrycook's in the High Street. One now has to step down into this shop (a wool shop) to the old level of Low Street.

FIREMEN AND AN ESCAPE outside the Royal Hotel.

A MUCH EARLIER FIRE BRIGADE.

FIREMAN FINNIS. A medal was awarded to him for gallant service at Cullens fire.

COASTGUARD CHIEF OFFICER JOHN BEDDELL.

COASTGUARD OFFICER WALDRON with rescue apparatus and crew.

Coastguard Station, Deal

THE COASTGUARD STATION, North Deal.

SHINGLE END COASTGUARD STATION.

EARLY FLYING, thought to be in the Sandhills.

EARLY DAYS in the Kent Coalfield – a group of miners at Northbourne 1 March 1913 engaged in boring for coal.

AN AERIAL VIEW OF BETTESHANGER COLLIERY, one of four in the Kent Coalfield all of which have now closed. The inauguration of Betteshanger Colliery took place on 19 May 1924. Lady Northbourne started the winding engine, lowering the Master and his men into the shaft to send out the first hoppit of chalk (E.C. Pain, *History of Deal*).

THE NATIONAL RESERVE on parade.

PEACE CELEBRATIONS at the Saracen's Head public house in Alfred Square.

A GROUP OF POSTMEN outside the post office in Park Street, 1901–4. Back row, left to right: W.H. Deanne (Town Postman); ? Featherstone, late entry; Steve Tyler (Rural Postman); Fred Hinds (who became Asst. Inspector); H.H. Chandler (recalled to Royal Navy 1914 and served in HMS *Lion* at Jutland); George Sidders (Head Postman). Front row, left to right: Wm. Dan Troot (who served in minesweepers during the war); Harry Sidders (Rural Postman and organist at Sholden Church); -?-, Frank James (Rural Postman) and Fred Sutton (Kingsdown). Good conduct brought an extra payment of one shilling weekly.

THE FIRST AID PARTY after the sinking of the *Dunbar Castle*. The messenger wearing the helmet, bottom right, is L. Hood.

THE ST JOHN'S AMBULANCE TEAM, proud winners of the Inter-Divisional Football Shield. Back row, right: Bobby Godfrey; front row, right: Tom Heard. The others have not been identified.

THE COACH 'CLARENCE' on a regular service between Deal and Dover, picking up passengers in South Street.

OFF ON AN OUTING in Marsh's Brake.

MOTORIZATION COMES TO KINGSDOWN – the local bus service from Deal, waiting at the Rising Sun in Kingsdown for passengers.

'FIVE DECADES OF BRITISH ELECTRIC TRACTION'. One of six buses transferred from Birmingham with which the Deal services were started in 1908.

THE BOARD ALONG THE BUS reads 'Deal & District Motor Services operated by the Birmingham and Midland Motor Omnibus Co. Ltd. Speed 12 m.p.h.' Dated 1908.

'BILL' ARNOLD, a member of the well-known local family, here very proud of his car, the first in Walmer.

EVERYONE STOPS TO HEAR THE NEWS from the Town Crier, shown here near the pier. Marsh's brake is in the background.

DONKEY RIDING along the sea front. Oatridges restaurant is in the background.

BEN BAILEY shaking out a fine haul of spratts in November 1951.

THREE OLD SALTS – Cookie, Budd and Kelly Baker.

ANOTHER MEMBER of the Arnold family at Kingsdown; the grandfather of our local journalist, Tony Arnold.

ON THE BEACH at the North End. Legend has it that the boy on the capstan is 'Long Jobber' Marsh.

WALTER MONK AND DICKIE PHILPOTT sorting bait. A pre-First World War photograph.

GEORGE BAKER (hands apart) and Mat Hoile in 1954.

THE SNAPPER SNAPPED. The gentleman with the camera is Basil Kidd, the local newspaper photographer, taking a picture to record the re-naming ceremony on 9 September 1971 of the Forester Public House. The tall gentleman to his left, Robin Brazier, was editor of *The Mercury*.

MR & MRS PRESTON, licencees of The Port Arms public house. Note the decorated pump handles.

JACK 'SPAINARD' MAY — a Deal Hoveller.

AN IVORY CARVING OF ELIZABETH CARTER, Deal's blue stocking. Born in 1717, the daughter of Dr Nicholas Carter a preacher of Canterbury Cathedral with a perpetual curacy at Deal, she was a friend of Dr Samuel Johnson. Her great claim to fame was her translation of *Epictetus* from the Greek. She died in London in 1806.

THE LICENCE granted to the Revd Nicholas Carter in the year 1718. The original is in St George's Church.

A LOVELY PICTURE – Deal coastguard 'Nigger' Brown with his bride on their wedding day in 1904.

EDWARD BRITTENDEN with his wife and family, 1914.

R.G. WATERS MILK DEPOT at the north end of Liverpool Road, Walmer. Here taking part in a pageant 'Presenting 1935'.

REVD DAVID BRUCE PAYNE, Vicar of St George's Church.

THE FUNERAL PROCESSION to Walmer churchyard of Canon D. Bruce Payne.

ST GEORGE'S CHURCH in the snow.

THE MUCH LOVED AND RESPECTED REVD OWEN T. JONES, vicar of St George's Church and President of Deal Rotary Club 1970/71.

REVD JAMES B. BARKER, rector of St Andrews. This photograph was taken just five weeks before his death on 26 November 1892, aged 51 years.

ST ANDREW'S CHURCH.

FEBRUARY 1961. All telephonists of the Deal Exchange are present to bid farewell to Marjorie Sims of Manor Road who was emigrating to New Zealand.

POST OFFICE SPORTS AND SOCIAL CLUB, 1960, at the Astor Royal (now Rooks the butchers).

WALMER CUB SCOUTS, 1922.

SHOLDEN SCOUT HUT TRAMPS SUPPER in 1952. Bronc. Newing (bearded), Skipper Kimpton (with the bottle).

A GROUP OF BOWLERS. Deal is fortunate in having two very good bowling clubs.

STAFF OF LLOYDS BANK and Dover District Council Law & Administration Dept. at a charity football match in 1975, in aid of the British Heart Foundation.

WALMER INFANTS SCHOOL, 1919.

LAYING THE FOUNDATION STONE of Downs Primary School in 1969.

STANDARD II, Wesleyan School, around 1895.

GIRLS AT ST GEORGE'S SCHOOL in around 1905. The teacher was Miss Rogers.

'FEED MY LAMBS' – there was once a school in Middle Street.

NEW SCHOOL, Upper Deal, now St Leonard's Church Hall.

THE COVER of John Pittock's Catalogue, 1897.

THE BAKERY at Upper Walmer owned by Mr W.H. Wheeler.

HOOK & SON, Fruiterers.

A COALMAN, thought to be Mr Holmes of Water Street.

FOAD'S DAIRIES — farmed at Sutton. The milkman is James Henry Terry of Middle Street with Mary the horse.

PHILPOTT'S DELIVERY VAN.

REDSULL & SONS, furnishers and removers.

GEORGE NOBLE, a leather seller, outside his shop at No. 102 High Street, Deal.

MBERT'S (LATE DONOVAN'S) MODEL HAND LAUNDRY, DEA

urgest and most Up=to=date Hand Laundry in **DEAL** and the Neighbourhood
EXTENSIVE OPEN AIR DRYING GROUNDS.

ADVERTISING LAMBERT'S LAUNDRY in the 1909 Town Guide.

THE MOAT at Sandown Castle.

THE UNUSUAL PHENOMENON OF BEACH WELLS at the top of Capstan Row and, below, off Farrier Street.

ANOTHER WELL off Farrier Street. As can be seen, they were well constructed and were in all probability for domestic use by houses that were once built on the beach.

WARTIME SEA DEFENCES at Walmer, looking north from the Lifeboat House.

MORE WARTIME DEFENCES, along the beach at Walmer in 1940.

A CLOSER LOOK at the Heinkel which was landed on the beach 8 July 1940. The pilot was captured while taking photographs of our sea defences.

BOMB DAMAGE in Canada Road, Walmer.

SHELLING DAMAGE, The Strand, Walmer.

BLENHEIM ROAD after a raid on 18 August 1940.

MORE BOMB DAMAGE in Gladstone Road.

GLADSTONE ROAD after the raid on 18 August 1940, when Redsull's store was wrecked.

THE BOMBED OUT EAST KENT BUS GARAGE.

VE DAY celebrations in Foreland Square.

Club House, Cinque Ports Golf Club, Deal.

ROYAL CINQUE PORTS GOLF CLUB, Deal. The 7th Green. It is one of three championship golf courses in the area.

A LITTLE HAVEN OF PEACE — a corner of Victoria Park.

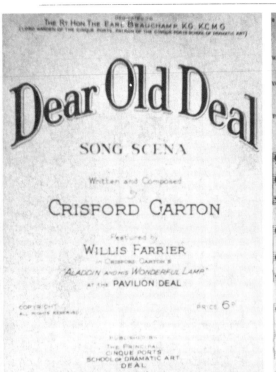

DEAL OLD DEAL — a song written and composed by Crisford Garton and sung by Willis Farrier in the pantomime *Aladdin and His Wonderful Lamp* presented by the Cinque Ports School of Dramatic Art at the Pavilion.

UPPER STREET, Kingsdown.

VILLA VITA, Kingsdown.

THE KINGS HEAD at Kingsdown – the dairy and a grocers shop were demolished, together with cow sheds and farm buildings.

SOUTH ROAD, Kingsdown, around 1903. The board at the bottom reads 'Post Office, D.D. Pittock – licensed to let landaus'.

NORTH STREET, Kingsdown, before development. Note the church standing alone at the top of the hill.

UPPER STREET, Kingsdown.

A NEOLITHIC HEARTH, discovered when preparing a site for building on the north-east side of Rectory Road, Upper Deal, in April 1970.

AN EXCAVATION AT WIRD HILL, Kingsdown, looking south. March 1971.